# The Course of Nature
A book of drawings on evolution and its consequences

*That many and grave objections may be advanced against the theory of descent with modification through natural selection, I do not deny. I have endeavoured to give to them their full force. Nothing at first can appear more difficult to believe than that the more complex organs and instincts should have been perfected not by means superior to, though analogous with, human reason, but by the accumulation of innumerable slight variations, each good for the individual possessor.*

Charles Darwin

*Any view of the Universe that is not strange is false.*

Neil Gaiman

# The Course of Nature

A book of drawings on evolution and its consequences

**Amy Pollack**

With commentary by Robert Pollack

**College of Arts and Letters**
Stevens Institute of Technology
Hoboken, New Jersey

12 13 14 7 6 5 4 3 2 1 FIRSTEDITION

ISBN: 978-1-58498-090-2

Book design by Summer Hart

Published in association with Jensen/Daniels,
an imprint of Talisman House, Publishers;
P.O. Box 896; Greenfield, Massachusetts 01302

*To the course of marriage:*
*Science and Art,*
*Charles and Emma Darwin,*
*and our own marriage of fifty years.*

# Table of Contents

**Introduction**
Lisa M. Dolling

**Preface**
Robert Pollack

**Drawings**
Amy Pollack

**Acknowledgements**

# Introduction

Lisa M. Dolling
Professor of Philosophy and Dean
College of Arts and Letters
Stevens Institute of Technology

*The aim of art is to represent not the outward appearance of things,
but their inward significance*

Aristotle, *Rhetoric*

*The aim of art is not to copy nature, but to express it.*

Honoré de Balzac, *The Unknown Masterpiece*

Few people would deny the importance of the work of Charles Darwin
or the impact that his theories have had on our understanding of history, nature,
and our place in the world. In fact, one would be hard pressed to find a theory
that has informed our collective consciousness as much as the theory of evolution. Which is why when it came time for the College of Arts and Letters (CAL)
at Stevens Institute of Technology to compile a list of works to include as part
of a new freshman seminar entitled *CAL Colloquium: Knowledge, Nature, Culture* – a
course intended to provide for all our students a broad overview of the human-
istic disciplines along with an appreciation for their value in navigating today's
social and moral issues – Darwin's *On the Origin of Species* was at the top of the list.
We unanimously agreed that there was no better way to give students a probing
insight into the development of history in the face of compelling scientific evidence and the ways we are then forced to rethink the very meaning of certain
concepts and ideas than a study of the work that forever changed the intellectual
landscape of human knowledge. Yet, inasmuch as the aim of our new course was
to introduce students to the humanities and social sciences, our primary goal in
having them read Darwin was to teach them about history, or perhaps the sociol-
ogy of ideas, and not necessarily biology.

Nevertheless, the more the faculty involved with this course discussed the
matter, the more we realized how essential an understanding of biology was for
a deeper appreciation of Darwin's revolutionary work; how an insight into the
details of things like adaptation, natural selection, genetic coding and mutation,
not to mention how the various natural processes worked, were a *sine qua non* for a
full comprehension of the theory of evolution and the lasting impact it has had on

our understanding of the course of nature and our place in it. But since we were all humanists, we could only hope our students would seek out such knowledge on their own. So when our dear friend and CAL advisor, Professor Robert Pollack, suggested that his wife Amy's drawings depicting "evolution and its consequences" be used as a companion to our course readings, we were delighted. Here before us was an opportunity not only to have the biology explained by one of the most renowned experts in the field, but to have it done in a way that would make use of a mode of presentation that is most relevant to CAL – that is, the work of art. It seemed that our partnership with the Pollacks on this project was a perfect – or as Bob likes to say, a "pre-adapted" – match.

The College of Arts and Letters at Stevens Institute of Technology is an academic unit particularly devoted to pursuing research and scholarship at the intersection of the arts, humanities, science, and technology. While it does seem that the traditionally opposed disciplines of art and science have been working together more productively in more recent years, it is unfortunately still the case that one continues to encounter that old sense of polarity and tension between them, whether in terms of the right brain vs. left brain, subjectivity vs. objectivity, symbolism vs. formalism, or that mainstay of the philosophy of science, understanding vs. explanation. Regardless of the form it takes, we at CAL have chosen as our pedagogic and scholarly mission to show the ways this opposition is no longer tenable, and how both art and science can enrich and enhance the understanding and appreciation of the other. Bringing together the drawings of artist/scientist Amy Pollack with the narrative of scientist/artist Bob Pollack has produced a work that is in many ways the very embodiment of the mission of our College and can serve as an exemplar for how we might achieve our goals. In that respect the Pollacks have provided us with a gift – a gift of their talents, their generosity, their wisdom and insights, and their inspiration. Allow me to say a word or two about how we were fortunate enough to become involved with the Pollacks and what led to our collaboration on *The Course of Nature*.

Many of us at the College of Arts and Letters first became aware of Amy Pollack's artistic talent when we had the good fortune to welcome Robert Pollack as one of our keynote speakers for a conference entitled "Science, Technology, and the Humanities: A New Synthesis." During his talk, entitled "Locating the Soul in an Age of Molecular Medicine," Professor Pollack used slides of some of Amy's drawings – many of which appear in the present volume – to help demonstrate his thesis. One such illustration that particularly delighted the entire audience was that of Alice and the Cheshire Cat, sitting atop a set of encyclopedias which were intended to represent the 13.7 billion years of time that have elapsed thus far. This wonderfully evocative drawing (which appears as Figure 5 below) shows us that in a set of 30 volumes, where each 450 page book represents 450 million years (1 page equalling 1 million years, with volume 1 adjusted to be a few pages longer), the first forms of life (archeobacteria) do not appear until sometime in volume 22. As if that were not enough to remind us of our insignificance in the grand scheme of things, Bob went on to explain that human life would not emerge until volume 30, finally appearing on the last tenth of the last page of the last volume. No doubt when one hears or reads the more formal explanation "we humans first appeared a few hundred thousand years ago" one is certainly intrigued and impressed, perhaps even jolted once one realizes that the universe had been in existence for more than 13.6 billion years prior to us. However, seeing this fact pictorially expressed using the imagery of books and information, not to mention size of scale and significance, gives one a special sort of pause. Indeed, many of us walked away from Bob's lecture still talking about how powerful those images found in Amy's drawings were, not only for their ability to explain the science, but to provide us with a reference point for reflecting on the wonder and mystery that science often conveys.

It is worth noting that when this illustration appears in the present work, Bob elaborates as follows: "And then, about sixty-thousand years ago, recorded somewhere toward the last sentence so far, would be the emergence in our species of language, texts, and, in that mental world, thoughts of imagined and imaginary creatures like the Cheshire Cat and Alice of *Alice in Wonderland....*" He then goes on to explain that the period punctuating that final sentence in the collection of all those thousands of pages represents all the time where "science has taken hold of our imaginations as a way to understand all this." Here too, we can "know" or "acknowledge" that modern science is a relatively recent achievement of humankind and thus only available to us for a short period of time; but to see that fact brought to life as an image, as Amy Pollack is able to do, gives it entirely new meaning.

Aware that Amy possessed this wonderful ability to be able to render such powerful ideas into images, we were thrilled when she agreed to provide us with a drawing for the cover of what was to become the textbook for our *CAL Colloquium*. As noted above this course was intended to introduce all Stevens students to the enduring importance of reading seminal classics in the humanities and social sciences, especially in terms of their value for forging an educated and meaningful existence. Once I provided Amy with the Introduction to our text of readings, she produced for us an illustration that that not only captured the essence of our course and what we hoped to achieve, but did so in a way that was wonderfully inviting to the reader, entreating him or her to embark on the journey into the world of ideas the course was intended to be. Above all Amy Pollack was able to depict for us through artistic imagery the importance and value of cultivating the life of the mind.

When Bob told me that Amy had produced an entire series of drawings that focused specifically on nature, life, and the "story" of evolution, I was delighted at the very thought of how these drawings must appear, imagining that just as with "Alice and the Encyclopedias" or the cover for our CAL reader, these illustrations would be able to entice one seriously to ponder things like natural selection, DNA, and heredity, making use of images that were equally evocative, accessible, and inviting as the ones we had seen. So when Bob asked my assistance in obtaining a publisher for the entire collection of Amy's drawings, we at CAL jumped at the chance!

The quantum physicist Niels Bohr once noted that both science and art are concerned with creating images – images that explain and express reality. That is precisely what Amy Pollack's drawings do. They express ideas and concepts that oftentimes cannot be fully captured by mere words. In that sense they are the perfect complement to scientific explanation. And as Bohr might further acknowledge, as complementary, both science and art are equally necessary for a full explanation of the natural phenomena. It is worth noting that Bohr further remarked that in the end, however arcane or even counterintuitive our scientific ideas might be, we must be able to explain them in terms of everyday language. The imagery that Amy Pollack uses in these drawings enables her to do exactly that. By taking notions and ideas from history, literature, art and architecture, culture and folklore, entertainment and everyday life, not to mention science itself, Amy has created works that summon the viewer to enter the world of scientific theory and think in ways that go beyond mere verbal explanation. Some of my favorite examples from the book are the following: the depiction of the smallness of a molecule in terms of the relationship of a mug of water to all the waters in the oceans; the rendering of the expansion of the universe or space-time continuum using the imagery of a balloon being continually blown up by no less than Einstein himself; the picturing of the folding of a growing amino-acid chain into a "three-dimensional machine" as various molecular origami figures; and, certainly one of the most compelling and evocative illustrations in the book, the explanation of the fact that the nucleus of any cell in a species contains a record of its ancestry using the depiction of the ancient Temple in the walled city of Jerusalem. In all, these images both capture the science, as well as lead one well beyond it.

Along those lines it is important to note that rather than view the artworks merely as accompanying illustrations for the textual explanation, the drawings in this book are meant to come first. As Bob notes in the Preface, it was his task "to elaborate on what each drawing instantaneously conveys." Therefore, the intention is that the reader start with a perusal of Amy's drawing and then go on to read the narrative that follows. The point is to spend time with the artistic renderings, reflecting on them a bit, immersing oneself in the richness and power of the ideas encoded in them, as one looks for clues to the scientific knowledge being revealed. Most important, as Bob remarked to me during one of our "editing" sessions, it is essential to bear in mind that the purpose of the drawings is not to "simplify down" the science but rather to "humanize it up."

It is in this last sense that this book holds the most value. It is a reminder that science too is a product of our human imagination. As the physicist Carl von Weisäcker once wrote, "Nature is prior to man; but man is prior to natural science," thus confirming that science and art require the same imaginative and creative inspiration and imagery to tell their stories; and that the story is the fullest when the worlds of art and science work together, lending depth and significance in ways that each one alone is unable to achieve. One must bear in mind that art can make us better scientists and science can make us better artists, and that taken together, both serve to make us better thinkers and knowers regarding the world and our place in it.

I would like to end by pointing to what was for me the most enriching and heartening aspect of *The Course of Nature*. That is the fact that despite conventional wisdom regarding the implications of Darwin's theory of natural selection when it comes to any sense of purpose in the world, after reading the Pollacks' work one is left instead with a keen appreciation of the uniqueness and wonder of human existence. In fact a central theme throughout this work is Bob Pollack's suggestion that a full understanding of biology reveals to us just how extraordinary human life is, as he declares that it confirms for us "what every person has always known from direct experience: every individual is equally rare and equally precious and should be treasured while they are with us. All of us are unimaginably rare, absolutely unique at birth." Moreover, *The Course of Nature* suggests that there is a potential irony inherent in the theory of evolution in what it reveals to us about free will; that is, as Bob explains, it is we who have the ability to exercise choice and thereby "bypass" natural selection "whether expressed through our mental activity or our capacity for joint action at the largest scales."

This fact about human existence is captured by Amy in what is probably my very favorite illustration of all. Appearing well toward the end of the book, we are shown a drawing of a "simple" record player. The record being played on it is meant to represent "the recording of life (that) has played out through the amplifier of natural selection for more than four billion years." While the illustration itself is rife with imagery and symbolism – especially in terms of the power of music – it is Bob's final statement regarding the uniqueness of being human that strikes an important chord for the significance of this work. He tells us that "our difference is, of course, that our mental capacities and our capacities for joint action do give us a unique extra capacity to control our future, a capacity we do not share with any other known creature on Earth. We are not merely a song on this record; we can make our own recordings." He then cautions us by declaring, "Let's hope we use that power wisely." I am confident that by studying *The Course of Nature*, our students will obtain the knowledge necessary to heed this wish and be inspired to compose their lives wisely, prudently, harmoniously, and, above all, in ways that make use of every sense of the term "love" that Bob outlines for us on the last page of his text.

*Lisa M. Dolling*
January, 2012

# Preface

Robert Pollack

What can we know about the whole Universe? What is life? How do we fit in? Do we have any freedom to choose how we act or is everything predictable? Every thinking person asks these questions, and for most of us the answers remain elusive. That's not because the questions are hard, nor because the answers are vague. It is because the answers we find hardest to toss away – the ones derived from experiment – are unexpected, unintuitive and really hard to accept.

I am a scientist, and Amy is an artist. We've had the good fortune to gain enough patience from each other to persist in confronting with the yearnings of our own hearts these facts that resist disproof. In the first decade of this new millennium the Stevens Institute of Technology College of Arts and Letters emerged. After getting to know the Dean of the College, Lisa Dolling, as well as many of the faculty members there, we found that it shared very much the same intentions that we had fostered all our lives.

When Dean Dolling invited Amy to create the cover art for the CAL reader described above, we all saw an opportunity to bridge a gap between art and science by putting together this book of Amy's drawings and my arguments, aimed at supplementing the CAL Colloquium reading by Charles Darwin. All that remained was for a *deus ex machina* to emerge with the funds to produce the book. When my colleague at Columbia University, Psychology Professor David Krantz, called Amy out of the blue to offer her a significant and unsolicited grant to publish her drawings this book needed only to be put together.

For that, my colleague at the Columbia University Seminars, Summer Hart, emerged as a master designer.

The format of the book is very simple. Each pair of facing pages has a drawing by Amy, and an explanation by me. My task has been to elaborate on what each drawing instantaneously conveys. We are hoping that the fun we have had with this mode of explanation in teaching will transfer to a book. To the extent it does, we welcome you to our world.

## Chapter 1
The course of nature, *Figures 1-12*

What do we know about the whole universe? What is its size, its duration, its future? Is there a part of it we know we cannot know? The universe has a history; life on Earth is a part of that larger history. DNA-encoded information lies in a self-copying string of chemical letters; its information for the design of a living thing can be stable enough to be inherited, yet capable of change at any time. The history of DNA-encoded life on Earth is not played out on an eternal stage, but is only one local example of the ways in which various parts of the Universe have changed since it began.

## Chapter 2
The course of true love, *Figures 13-24*

The genetic code: DNA information yields a set of machines called proteins, and the regulation of when and where these are to be made. Regulation of DNA expression may be different in each of the different cells of an organism. Sexual reproduction is an additional of source of differences in DNA: it picks one DNA sequence from two choices at every generation. Life has persisted since it began on Earth, while constantly changing over time, always becoming diverse, and always subject to the penalty of individual death. A population that includes all individuals capable of fertile mating with each other is called a species. Life today is found in hundreds of millions of different species.

## Chapter 3
The course of evolution, *Figures 25-34*

Why this many species? Why has life not generated more species, or acquired one single, stable, form? The positive feedback loop of survival of information in DNA explains this. Information in the sequence of base-pairs in a DNA may – but need not – include instructions for the successful copying and persistence of itself. The subsequent differential survival of DNA sequences that contribute best to their own survival generates a tree of ancestral relationship among all forms of life alive today. Darwin's insight into our origins came a century before DNA was discovered. Darwin read the evidence from fossils to be consistent with all current species having been descended from now-dead ancestral species. Darwin's deepest insight: the more that similar parts of any two species differ from each other, the longer ago their last common ancestor must have died off. DNA evidence provides a complete mechanism to explain Darwin's vision that the origin of species is descent from ancestral species with modification subject to natural selection.

## Chapter 4
The course of human events, *Figures 35-40*

What parts of our species does natural selection explain, and what parts are beyond it? Can a chemical form of life have free will? The positive selection in our species for novel sequences that delay the maturation of the brain offers the beginning of an answer. Our intrinsic sociability and our specific language capacity are both built upon our specific extended helplessness during infancy through very early childhood. Our DNA does not encode our minds, and so any human brain can have any idea. Two implications of the biological capacity for free will are that we have no DNA to blame for our actions, and that it is never too late to change our minds. What then is to be done?

# Chapter 1

**Figure 1**

Life covers the planet Earth, but barely. We can find living things a few miles deep into the oceans, and a few miles up into the atmosphere, and on the surface of all land. But our planet has a diameter that measures in the thousands of miles. The part of Earth that holds life, called the biosphere, is restricted to a very thin wrapping that lies over, on and in the Earth. So far as we know, that wrapping is the entirety of life's presence in the Universe. We may think of ourselves as dominating the planet, but the reality is that especially to the extent that we dominate it, we must somehow continue to fit into this thin membrane on a planet, a membrane fragilely balanced to permit our existence. How thin is it?

When dealing with very large differences in size or any other measure, it is useful to have a language of approximation. We can easily round off a measurement in any units to the nearest factor of ten. Since our number system adds a digit to the size of a number every time it increases by ten-fold, we can reduce the measurement to the number of zeroes in it. This is called the exponent: $10^6$ is shorthand for 1 with six zeroes after it, or a million. By convention, $10^0$ is 1. So, $10^9$ is 1,000,000,000, that is, a billion. That's a thousand times bigger than a million, which is $10^6$ or 1,000,000; a million times bigger than $10^3$ which is 1,000 or a thousand; and a billion times bigger than $10^0$ or 1. Quantities smaller than 1 have negative exponents. So, in terms of exponents, the biosphere's thickness is only about $1/1,000$, or $10^{-3}$, times the diameter of the Earth

Rounded to the nearest factor of ten, and using scientific units, a typical apple is on the order of 10 centimeters in diameter, and its peel is no more than a tenth of a centimeter, or 1 millimeter, thick. That means that the ratio of the peel to the apple is about $10/0.1$, or $10^{-2}$. That is ten times thicker relative to the apple, than the thickness of the biosphere is, relative to Earth.

Only six of the elements found in and on the surface of the Earth make up almost all of the material of the living world: hydrogen, oxygen, carbon, sulfur, phosphorus and nitrogen. Why is life so prolific within the constraints of this thin membrane, and so absent elsewhere? Because life is made of atoms, and since atoms are so small, life can be made of complicated sets of atoms assembled into very improbable structures; life on Earth turns out to have needed these atoms, and the temperatures found only this thin membrane.

Is there life elsewhere in the Universe? Would it be subject to these constraints? We do not know.

# Figure 2

How small are atoms? We know very little about Titus Lucretius Carus: he was born in Rome about 100 BCE, died before he was fifty, and left us only one long poetic essay, *On the Nature of Things*. In that poem Lucretius tries to ease the fear of death by imagining a universe composed entirely of invisibly tiny objects. He calls these atoms, to indicate that they are also irreducible [a-tom/no-parts]. Everything, Lucretius says, is just a particular, temporary local assembly of atoms that fill the universe. Nothing, he says, is anything but one or another such arrangement. On death, the arrangement that is a life simply ends, and the atoms of it go to form other structures.

About a hundred years ago – only two thousand years later – scientists testing their ideas about the structure of matter became pretty confident Lucretius had got it at least partly right. All parts of the Universe we can detect - the living and the rest - are made of atoms and the forces that hold atoms together or repel them from each other. Real atoms are divisible into smaller parts though; atomic energy and atomic weapons both use that ironic fact.

There are more than a hundred different kinds of atoms, each made of a tiny nucleus holding almost all of the atom's mass, surrounded by a relatively large, spherical cloud of electrons. How small are atoms relative to anything we can see with our own eyes? The smallest unit of distance on a common ruler is the millimeter; that's one tenth of a centimeter, or about one twentieth of an inch. The diameter of an atom is approximately $10^{-7}$ millimeter; this means atoms are small enough for ten million of them to be lined up in a row inside that smallest unit of the ruler.

Here's another way to look at how small atoms are. A molecule of water is made of two hydrogen atoms and an oxygen atom, held together by the sharing of their electron clouds: $H_2O$. If you take a large mug, one that holds about ten ounces, and fill it with water, it will have about $10^{25}$ molecules of water in it.

It would require about $5 \times 10^{21}$ mugs of water, each with $10^{25}$ molecules of water, to fill all the oceans on Earth. So, there are thousands of times more molecules of water in a single mug, than there are mugs of water in all the oceans of the world. Rounding to the nearest exponent, $10^{25}$ molecules per mug divided by about $10^{22}$ mugs in all oceans equals about $10^3$ times more molecules in one mug than mugs in all the oceans.

So if you were to fill that mug from any ocean, pour it back, mix thoroughly with all the oceans, and then dip and fill the mug again, you'd be certain of getting a few thousand of the water molecules from the first mug, in the mug the second time. That's how small the atoms are that make a single molecule of water, or of any other part of the universe.

# Figure 3

How many atoms in a person? We are made of about $10^{14}$ cells. Each of them is made of about $10^{15}$ atoms. This means there are about $10^{29}$ atoms in any one of us.

We may reasonably have some difficulty in imagining such small sizes and such large quantities. Here, a royal personage is holding the yardstick by which all measurements are compared. He is the Ruler of that ruler, and so the yard is a measure of his own anatomy – from his nose to his outstretched hand.

His robes carry the subversive message of his unimportance, his smallness, relative to the very large number of atoms of which he is assembled. That is a fact that resonates with the irony of the atoms Lucretius predicted being very much divisible into their constituent parts.

The diameter of an atom's nucleus is only one part in 100,000, or $10^{-5}$, of the diameter of its cloud. The volume of an atom is therefore the cube of that ratio, or approximately $10^{15}$, or a million trillion times greater than the volume of its nucleus. A single atom in turn, is only one part in $10^{15}$ of a single cell in the royal body.

What about cells and bodies?

A single human cell is only one part in $10^{15}$ of – no, not the royal personage alone – but a social group of about ten people; a jury, say, or a family. This coincidence of ratios serves to tell us that no person is truly alone for very long. We cannot emerge from infancy alone, nor can we expect to become fully human in isolation.

In recent years a second and somewhat disconcerting fact about ourselves and our bodies has emerged from research into the causes of certain diseases. Not even our bodies are alone: during the nine months of gestation, each person and his or her mother exchange cells across the placenta.

Enough of these cells survive for decades to assure that each of us is in fact a mosaic of cells from at least two different people. Every mother carries some living cells from each of her children, and every child carries some living cells from his or her mother.

# Figure 4

Now that we have a sense of where we are in the universe in terms of size relative to the size of an atom, how about in terms of time, relative to the time the Universe has existed? Even to ask that question is to open the door to one of the strangest aspects of our Universe, the notion that time and space themselves both began at a single point and at a single time.

The data we have, together with fairly well-established astrophysical theories based on Einstein's general relativity theory, strongly suggest that there was an instant about 13.7 billion – that is, approximately $10^{10}$ – years ago at which both time and space began as a singularity, a point containing all of space. So everyone's first questions – what was around that point and what was before it? – are impossible to answer. There was no "around," nor was there a "before." At that point, everything was there, and time had just begun.

How did things get from that instant to here and now? To begin with, as time began that point expanded far more rapidly than the speed of light. As it expanded, the average temperature of the universe cooled down enough to permit the parts of atoms to assemble, and then to be clustered together by an attractive force – gravity – that draws any collection of atoms to each other in proportion to their masses.

Even as gravity pulled together the first stars and then clumped them into the first galaxies, the universe itself, what Einstein called the "space-time continuum," continued to expand and is expanding even now. We are constantly getting further away from all other parts of the Universe not because we are traveling away, but because with its expansion, the distances between any two parts of the Universe become bigger. We are in the three-dimensional version of what dots on the surface of a balloon experience as the balloon is being blown up.

Another great and wholly unintuitive insight of Einstein, borne out by decades of observation: while the universe is expanding much faster than the speed of light, nothing within the space – time continuum itself can go faster than the speed of light. This caps our ability to know how big the universe may have gotten since the initial moment. We are sitting at the center of a sphere of light that has come to us at that limiting speed since the first instant, and any objects that might be situated further away than light could have traveled since that initial instant, are simply barred from our view.

Within this sphere of knowability, we can see approximately $10^{11}$ galaxies with approximately $10^{11}$ stars in each. So now, as we sit here on Earth, each of us made of ~ $10^{29}$ different atoms inside of a $10^{10}$ year-old universe of no fewer than $10^{22}$ suns, the big question this raises is, when is "now?"

That depends on where you are: there is no single "now" that we can speak of except in our imaginations. In reality, we are separated by the time it takes for light to get from one of us to the other. A Mars Rover's "now" is many minutes behind our own here on Earth, and when we sit around a table, each of us has a "now" that is a nanosecond or so ahead of the "now" of our tablemates.

# Figure 5

We sit today on a rocky, metallic planet composed of the atoms of dead stars, orbiting a middle-aged star born of the same stardust some 5 billion years ago. We share the gift of an imagination capable of creating and remembering creatures that never were in nature like Alice and the Cheshire Cat, first drawn more than a century ago by Tenniel for Lewis Carroll's *Alice in Wonderland*. Our sun may live another 5 or 10 billion years but no more. It is held by gravity in an arm of a galaxy born some ten billion years ago, in a universe born some 13.7 billion years ago.

Imagine the approximately 13.7 billion years since the beginning of space-time as being recorded in a set of books. If each book had 450 pages, and each page were to record a million years, then each volume would be the passage of 450 million years, and 30 volumes would come out to be 13.5 billion years. If we let the first volume have 650 pages, it will allow the whole library stack in the drawing to be a record of 13.7 billion years of time passing in that part of the universe where we are now.

The sun and the earth both formed by gravity from the stuff of exploded stars – the atoms of the elements – some time recorded on the pages of volume 18. The bindings on each volume are an index of the kinds of life that were here in the periods they represent. From volume 1 to volume 20 – that is, for times from the beginning of everything until a bit more than nine billion years later, or about 5 billion years ago – there is nothing on any of the bindings, which is to say there was no sign of life on earth at all for all those billions of years.

But let's be patient. After all, our galaxy is not more than ten billion years old, and our sun not older than 5 billion, which would put its formation, along with the formation of the Earth, at some time that we record in volume 18. So there's no reason to expect any annotation on any binding until that volume. Seen that way, life on Earth was a rather rapid development. Its beginnings may not have left chemical or physical evidence, but only a billion years after the Earth cooled down from its formation the first fossils did appear.

Archeobacteria, the first forms of life, appeared in the seas in the period recorded in volume 22. Their least-changed descendants still thrive in deep-ocean vents, where the heat and the gases emerging from the Earth's mantle provide the environment that most closely resembles the Earth at the time of their first appearance.

**Figure 6**

Bacteria living deep in the sea would continue to be the only shape life took for another billion years, taking up the time recorded in volumes 23 and 24. Then about two billion years ago the energy of the sun's light was captured for food by a sea-borne bacterium that used that energy to strip the atom carbon from the molecule carbon dioxide, building more of itself from the carbon while releasing oxygen as waste product. Photosynthesis, as it is called, changed the planet. Since that time, the oxygen levels of our atmosphere are at 20%, while the levels of oxygen on our neighboring planets are well under 1%.

With oxygen available as a source of energy, sunlight, which had been unnecessary for the archeobacteria, also became unnecessary for a new kind of ocean-living bacteria that was able to break down dead stuff and build more of themselves from it, using the energy of oxygen in a living, warm, stable version of fire, called aerobic metabolism. For these first two billion years of life aerobic, photosynthetic, and archeobacteria proliferated in the sea, their diversity being played out in their metabolisms, not in their shapes. About two billion years ago, at a time recorded in volume 25, the benefits of cooperation gave a new, much larger kind of cell a chance to proliferate. An archeobacterium engulfed an aerobic bacterium within itself, and the two lived happily ever after. The aerobic bacterium and its descendants were so effective at generating useful energy for the archeobacterium that the latter grew to a thousand-times larger volume, and its closely-held aerobic bacteria became mitochondria within its cell body, a permanent source of energy for the new, bigger kind of cell, and its descendants.

A second engulfment by an archeobacterium of a photosynthetic bacterium led to the appearance of the green version of this sort of big cell, with mitochondria, but also with the green descendants of the photosynthetic bacterium, called chloroplasts. Volumes 25 and 26 record the billion years or so when other big-celled forms of life like paramecia and diatoms joined these first big cells, and life became a mixture of sea-going big and little cells, photosynthetic, aerobic and archeobacteria.

# Figure 7

Big cells soon gained the capacity for a more complicated, social form of existence. By the times recorded in volume 27, a billion and a half years ago, sponges and other simple multicellular forms of life appeared in the seas. And then, organisms made from many big cells whose ancestry was newly complicated appeared: each had two parents, and each began as a single large cell formed by the fusion of a sperm and egg cell. This new way of making the next generation began in the sea, then found its way onto land, taking its place in, on and under the planet in a formidable Bayeux Tapestry of conquest by different life forms.

One sort of sexual creature, with a different head and bottom but with mirror-symmetric left and right sides, and with a symmetric backbone and four legs, appeared some time in the period recorded in volume 29, less than a billion years ago. Other four-limbed creatures, tetrapods as we call them and as we might call ourselves after all, climbed out of the seas and occupied parts of the surface of the Earth not that long ago, well within the last billion years. And so opened the period recorded in the current volume, 30.

In the times recorded in the current volume, volume 30, big animals and plants, each following the sexual habit of having two parents, thrived for the period represented by the first 250 pages, until the great Permian-Triassic extinction, brought on by an undefined disaster of literally cosmic proportions, wiped out about 90% of all organisms alive to that moment. The survivors prevailed for another period represented by another 185 pages worth of time, until about 65 million years ago an asteroid struck the Yucatan peninsula. It so disrupted the Earth's land, water and air that all large life forms – including the dinosaurs, alas – were wiped out. Among the tetrapods that survived were small, flying dinosaurs whose closest relatives we know today as birds, and small, hairy creatures who raised their young on mothers' milk, the mammals.

We humans appeared in Africa a few hundred thousand years ago. A note about our emergence would be on the last tenth of the last page of that last volume. And then, about sixty-thousand years ago, recorded somewhere toward the last sentence so far, would be the emergence in our species of language, texts and, in that mental world, thoughts of imagined and imaginary creatures like the Cheshire Cat and Alice of *Alice in Wonderland*. The period punctuating that last sentence would represent the past few hundred years, and so it would bring us to the present moment. The width of that simple dot records the time since science has taken hold of our imaginations as a way to understand all this.

How has the part of nature we call life managed to be so creative, so diverse, and so complicated over 4 billion years, able to overcome even asteroid impacts? How is it that life today is made up of so many different fertile species, each a separate population of individuals that – or in our case, who – can make babies with one another, and whose babies can make babies in turn?

# Figure 8

There's a single, if strange, answer to both questions. The path to it is to ask what could have happened between the formation of the Earth and Sun in times recorded in volume 18, and the appearance of the first bacterial life forms whose fossils we can identify, in later times recorded in volume 22?

Whatever it was, it had to have happened using the materials of nature – the atoms that Lucretius imagined – and those materials had to assemble in some way that would permit information to be stored in them, and for that information to be copied, indefinitely. Otherwise we do not really have any way to understand the history we find recorded in these fossils, that is, the survival of so many forms of life for very long times, much longer than the lifetimes of any individual.

We do not have to look hard to find an example today of survival of information through chemical structures that use the atoms and forces of the universe. We need only look at a snowflake. Each snowflake is famously unique, though each has an overall similarity of shape; they are almost all six-sided. Snowflakes begin as tiny crystals of ice that condense and freeze from the moistness in cold air. Depending on local temperature and humidity water freezes directly from water vapor into one of two hexagonal shapes, a flat six-sided plate, or a long, six-sided prism.

Each snowflake is different, because each has fallen from the sky through a unique pathway of slightly varying temperature and humidity. As a result each of its six sides grows out in a unique pattern of plates and prisms. And because the history of the flake is similar for all six sides, all six sides will take on the same unique pattern. So a snowflake wears its history in its shape, all of it inherited from its immediate past. It passes the first test for an inherited history in a chemical form.

What about survival of the information after the death of the individual snowflake? Is it alive? When a snowflake dies by melting, nothing is left of that history; it is lost forever. Friends from Alaska tell of the great sadness they feel as their glaciers melt and recede in this period of global warming. In that case it is not just a snowflake's structure that is lost, but also the gigantic aggregate mass of many snowflakes over many centuries.

The novelty of a snowflake cannot ever become the source of any form of historical memory longer-lived than itself. But persistent chemical memory of the past is the very hallmark of all of the forms of life that have filled the times recorded in the last ten volumes of our library in an unbroken persistence of complex life forms. What have all these current and past forms of life got that a snowflake doesn't have? Information.

In *On the Nature of Things,* Lucretius writes "Therefore, the supposition that, as there are many letters common to many words so there are many elements common to many things, is preferable to the view that anything can come into being without elementary particles." That takes us to DNA.

# Figure 9

What sort of vine is this person climbing? Some time in the period recorded in volume 21 a molecule called DNA came together as an assembly of atoms of the sort Lucretius was so prescient about. This molecule is still with us today because of the singular pair of properties it had and still has. It carries information in a sequence of 4 letters. In that DNA is just like any other text. But unlike any text in other languages, these letters are assembled from only a few dozen atoms each. And unlike other text, DNA has the capacity to act at once as both book and scribe, making copies of itself.

DNA is assembled from only 5 of the 92 elements that occur naturaly on Earth: carbon, phosphorus, hydrogen, oxygen and nitrogen. It is a molecule that always takes the same shape: a long skinny twisted pair of molecular vines. Each vine is made of repeats of molecules assembled from phosphorus, hydrogen and oxygen (the "NA" of "DNA," shorthand for "Deoxyribose Nucleic Acid"). Repeatedly jutting off each string is a stem of the sugar Deoxyribose (the D of DNA) made of carbon, hydrogen and oxygen.

Attached to each sugar stem is one of four possible flat molecular leaves made of carbon, nitrogen, oxygen and hydrogen, called cytosine, guanine, thymine and adenine. As the intrepid climber has just noticed, the two vines of double-stranded DNA are held together by pairs of leaves.

Not just any pairs of leafy bases will do. Only two pairs are seen. The same is true in DNA. The molecular versions of these leaves are abbreviated by the Latin letters C, G, T and A. Wherever there is a G on one strand, the other base must be a C, and wherever there is an A on one strand, the other base must be a T. The leaves reflect the molecular flatness of all four bases, which allows the two base-pairs to be flipped over so that they may be present as any of four base-pairs, G-C, C-G, A-T and T-A. These four may sprout from the two vines in any order, without disrupting their minimalist, smooth double-helical outer structure.

While the overall shape of a molecule of DNA has not changed for around 4 billion years, the order of the bases within that molecule may have changed innumerable times. So one may not say of two different DNAs that they are either the same or that they are different. They are both: their shape is the same, but the sequence of base pairs in them may be entirely different.

Since the sequence of a set of four possible letters carries information in proportion to the length of that string, we may say that for four billion years DNA has kept its form while encoding immeasurably large numbers of different texts. But how does a chemical go about copying itself?

# Figure 10

The discovery that DNA could have a structure which was textual and self-copying was reported in April 1953 as a 900 word prose-poem disguised as a letter to *Nature*. The authors were from different backgrounds but with a common interest in genetics. The very young American postdoctoral fellow and classical biologist James D. Watson, and the somewhat older British biophysicist Francis Crick, made quite a pair themselves.

The paper, titled "Molecular Structure of Nucleic Acids," opens with a classic British understatement: "This structure has novel features which are of considerable biological interest." That's British for: "You'll be amazed; no insight like this has appeared in print since Lucretius two thousand years ago."

Watson and Crick wrote that because others had found clear X-ray crystallographic patterns from a preparation of DNA, the sugar-phosphate backbones separating the base-pairs have to run in opposite directions. Otherwise, a "crystal" of DNA would be a random assortment of molecules running one way and others running the other way, and no clear pattern would emerge.

They then drew an astonishing inference from earlier work of other, less biologically oriented, chemists: of all possible combinations of bases, only an A-T pair and a G-C pair had precisely the same distance to the two backbones.

Weaving these insights into the work of other scientists, they argued not only is the sequence of base-pairs unrestricted by the structure of DNA, but also for the same reason, that the two strands are informationally redundant. And this, they argued, made DNA a candidate to be the chemical of inheritance, saying that even the inheritance of forms through time may be the property of an assembly of atoms.

Watson and Crick take their place as the formulators of this astonishing hypothesis. In figure 10 they sit as if they were in an Egyptian stele. Their bodies seem to resemble chromosomes, and the crisscrossed dots of the crystallographic pattern of a double helix are all about. Consider, they argued in *Nature*, what would be possible if the two strands separated, as they do here above each of their heads.

Each strand would be able to become the parent of a new double-stranded DNA. That new DNA would have precisely the same sequence of base-pairs as the one they are holding because in each case only the correct base to form a base-pair could go into the assembly of the new strand. This would finally yield two copies of the sequence of the DNA, each with one old strand and one new strand; this is called semiconservative replication.

Hovering over Watson and Crick and embraced by the old strands about to be made into copies of the DNA below are Rosalind Franklin and her lab director, Maurice Wilkins. Franklin, who died of ovarian cancer in 1958 at age 37, obtained the crucial crystallographic photos of DNA that were the basis for Watson and Crick's structural models. Wilkins, who oversaw the crystallographic study of DNA, shared the 1962 Nobel prize with Watson and Crick.

# Figure 11

Redundancy is the key to self-copying. Separate the two strands, and allow each to form a second strand by base-pairing, and you will always get precisely two copies of the same DNA. This is so because no matter the sequence of bases on either strand to begin with, whenever there's a T on one strand of a double-stranded DNA there will be an A on the other, wherever there's a G on one strand there will be a C on the other.

Each of the two copies will have one ancestral strand, and each will have one new strand. But each will have the same, ancestral, sequence of base-pairs, and therefore the same information will be passed on through time, indefinitely, for times longer than the chemical lifetime of the original DNA molecule.

The odd coinage "semi-conservative" refers to a possible disparity in the ages of the two stands: one must always be new with every DNA generation, but the other strand may – albeit with decreasing probability over time – be made with a backbone that has survived through any number of semi-conservative replications.

In this drawing a DNA molecule slips its way through the double-helical constriction of an hourglass, marking off the time since it was made from an ancestral strand and a set of new subunits. Nothing chemical prevents the existence today of a molecule of DNA, one of whose backbones may be billions of years old. All that would be required for a DNA with such an ancient backbone to slip through time indefinitely, would be that it happen to remain inside a living organism, and not be lost altogether to death. DNA is a source of astonishing stability in preserving information through time.

Semi-conservative replication resolves what had been a total mystery until its discovery. How can a chemical contain information and yet be supple enough to carry the same information through any number of generations of copying? As Watson and Crick put it, "it has not escaped our notice that the specific pairing we had postulated immediately suggests a possible copying mechanism for the genetic material."

# Figure 12

But mistakes can happen. Let's follow what happens when DNA copying makes a mistake. For example, what would happen after two DNA strands separated, if one of the two new double-stranded copies put in a C opposite to an A, instead of putting a T there?

The C-A "pair" would be a counterfeit unable to assemble the two backbones properly. But that is not quite right: they would cause the new DNA to fail to maintain its absolute fidelity to the form of an undeviating double helix. Mistakes happen; how is it that DNA escapes these mistakes? Consider this remarkable possibility: that included in the information encoded in a stretch of base-pairs, one may find information that helps copy the DNA itself.

The Egyptian scribe in figure 12 is an enactment of that idea. Encoded by the DNA he copies, he personifies that use of the information in a DNA sequence. He is not passing on the text with absolute veracity; the DNA encoding him has not encoded perfection. He can detect his mistake and correct it, repairing the C-A typo. But there are two ways for him to make that correction: returning to the T-A base-pair, or "fixing" it by leaving the C and building from it a C-G base-pair.

Putting in a T for the C restores A-T base pair; the new DNA has a sequence identical with its ancestral backbone, and all is well. Putting in G for the A, however, does something radically different: it puts back a proper base-pair and the DNA is as sound as one could ask, but the sequence of bases has been changed!

Changes in base-pair sequence are called mutations. There's a common misperception that mutations are bad, or weak, or failures. In fact, they are merely textual novelties and only time tells what the consequence of the mutation will be to the DNA.

As a text, DNA must in some fashion be able to encode information for its own copying, with the risk of novelty. Novelty – mutation – may be a typo that has no effect on the meaning of the DNA text, or one that ends the meaningfulness of the text, or one that adds a new meaning to the text. Of all new meanings, the most significant must be the novelty in text that becomes a new way for the DNA to enhance its own copying.

We can tell these different novelties apart by reading the DNA the way it is read in nature.

That brings us to chapter 2.

# Chapter 2

**Figure 13**

DNA is a text. Using a 4-letter alphabet of base-pairs it encodes information in its base-pair sequence in a manner identical to the way this sentence is encoding information using most of the 26 Latin letters and typographical symbols like the spaces between words and the period at the end of itself.

How is it read? To answer we have to look in more detail at how DNA encodes the meaningfulness of its text. We know it must encode information for the construction of some sort of machinery to carry out very specific chemical changes. Among those machines, we would certainly expect to find ones to copy the DNA itself by separating the strands, then sewing in the completed second strands to make two copies of DNA from one.

In addition, somehow the DNA must encode the turning on and off of these machines, in time and in space. This other sort of information encoded by the DNA is more subtle, and it is not yet fully understood. The machinery will be a protein, the switching is what we call regulation. Any single stretch of DNA that encodes both a single protein and the switches for turning on and off the production of that protein is called a gene.

Our ability to study gene regulation is relatively new. For some time the classic gene was thought of as simply the stretch of DNA that encoded a protein. We now understand that all living things including humans are built from proteins encoded by genes which are subject to gene regulation that is also encoded in our DNA.

The process of protein synthesis begins with transcription from the DNA of a version of nucleic acid that can carry a sequence from DNA out into the world. The two strands of DNA that encompass a gene are first separated from one another by other proteins encoded elsewhere, which provide the machinery for the process. Then a short, single-stranded molecule, called messenger RNA, is made by base-pairing to one of the strands.

Messenger RNA is very much like a single strand of DNA, but with a small chemical difference in the sugar backbone and with the base called T replaced by another base called U. When the messenger RNA is fully copied, it is released from the DNA which then re-seals as a double-helix.

Figure 13 is a drawing of transcription in the Classical Greek mode with the messenger RNA receiving a gift from an eternal Greek goddess, in this case the gift of the information in a stretch of a long-lived DNA sequence.

# Figure 14

Messenger RNA is subject to censorship: regulation may mean that it is cut to bits before anything further can be done with it. But when it is allowed by regulation to be handed off, it is quickly bound to a big machine made of many proteins and RNAs called the ribosome. Firmly attached there, it is then decoded, as its specific sequence of bases is converted into a corresponding sequence of amino-acids.

Amino acids are a family of molecules in which a single carbon atom links three elements: an amino group, $NH_2$; an carboxyl group, $O=C-OH$ (characteristic of organic acids); and a third group that determines which element of the amino-acid family is in question. In the simplest and smallest amino acid, glycine, this third group is just a hydrogen atom, but in other amino acids it can be complex, including several carbon and hydrogen atoms and perhaps also additional oxygen, nitrogen or sulfur.

Two or more amino acids can be linked in sequence, head-to-tail (amino group to carboxyl group), to form a chain. Short chains are called peptide molecules, while proteins, such as hemoglobin, consist of long chains of hundreds, sometimes even thousands of amino acids.

The genetic code translates a sequence from the alphabet of the 4 base-pairs into a corresponding sequence from another alphabet of 20 distinct amino acids. The code uses three-letter sequences of bases. Since there are $4^3$ or 64 possible three-letter sequences, there is plenty of room to encode 20 distinct amino acids.

Even as the growing amino-acid chain is not yet finished being translated it begins to fold up into a three-dimensional machine, like a molecular origami. The emergence of such a three-D, functional protein completes the translation of the meaning of a DNA sequence from the language of DNA base-pairs to the language of a sequence of amino-acids.

While every protein will emerge from folding up as a single machine, any living thing big enough to be seen will be made of tens of thousands of different kinds of proteins, each interacting with many of the others.

In figure 14 the folding of the molecular origami of an amino-acid chain attains the completion of the form of the organism that made it, whether bird or fish or frog.

# Figure 15

As a new string of amino-acids is forged on the ribosome, the final folding of the completed protein turns out to be a very elegant event. Different stretches of the nascent protein start folding on their own into one or another of a very small number of characteristic structures. These local origamis are called domains.

It is odd to find the same domains in so many different proteins, which raises the serious problem of likelihood. Given the enormous number of possible DNA sequences and therefore of amino-acid sequences why would sequences encoding domains be so common in proteins?

More surprising still, between the folded domains are often stretches of amino-acids that are flaccid, flexible, and undertake no specific folding at all. This allows the protein itself to assemble from its various domains into a single machine with a specific function.

The final function of the protein – a train in this figure – emerges first from the folding of the separate domains, then from the assembly of those domains into the finished protein.

# Figure 16

A messenger RNA can be transcribed from only one of DNA's two strands. One of the two DNA strands here each encodes a sentence in English, made of two sets of three bases, separated by a single base: ACT A CAT, TAG A CAT and GAG A CAT. Each is immediately translated – by us – into a meaningful sentence in English. But remember, to translate a DNA sequence into an amino-acid sequence takes an extra step before meaning emerges. That step is the transcription of one strand of the DNA into a messenger RNA.

The DNA strands we read in English are actually meaningless even in DNA's terms, because the messenger RNA each would produce would have a complementary base-pair sequence, and any protein would be encoded by that complementary RNA sequence, not by the direct DNA sequence we read in English.

If three messengers were to be transcribed from the complementary DNA strands for the sake of an English translation, they would read ACU A CAU, UAG A CAU, and GAG A CAU. Phonetically the first of these is tough to say, but we could imagine the second of these as an order to wag a cow, and the third as asking that we gag a cow.

Let these last two RNA-English sentences be enough to remind us that there is no shortcut around transcription of a messenger RNA to get to the final step of translation, where sets of three RNA bases each encode a different amino acid. A single-stranded, disposable and evanescent messenger RNA must carry the information from the DNA, information that upon translation becomes the folded protein's final function.

Why this added step? One current idea is that the RNA step is a molecular fossil from an RNA world, a time before DNA itself emerged from RNA by precisely the sort of creative error that mutations are capable of causing.

# Figure 17

The genetic code is drawn out here in the manner of the Rosetta Stone. That lexicon was carved in Egypt about 2300 years ago when Egypt was a Greek colony under Ptolemy. The Stone, a remnant of a stele, was recovered by a French expedition a little more than two hundred years ago. It was taken by the British as spoils of war a few years later and is now residing in the British Museum.

The Rosetta Stone was named by the French in a rather poor phonetic translation of the location it was dug from near the Egyptian city of Rashid. The same text was carved into the Rosetta Stone three ways. At the bottom is a body of text in Greek, the language of Egypt at the time it was carved. The middle text uses the demotic Egyptian alphabet and vocabulary to spell out the same meaning. At the top of the Rosetta Stone ancient hieroglyphs were used to make the same text a third time.

Similarly we can read this drawing from the bottom up beginning with the DNA text of a protein-coding sequence having already been transcribed into a messenger RNA, here separated into the triplets of bases that encode different amino acids. Remember, a stretch of DNA encoding a messenger RNA is a necessary, but not a sufficient requirement for a gene. A gene must also contain other stretches of DNA that encode the switches that turn its transcription of a message on or off as needed, depending on where the DNA finds itself in space and time during the life of the organism.

In the middle panel of the drawing, each triplet of RNA bases is translated into the particular amino acid it encodes. The names of the amino acids have been abbreviated to make the drawing legible; in full, they would be "phenylalanine valine cysteine ..."

Both the bottom and middle panels show fragments of text. The text at the bottom contains only 35 of the 64 possible triplets of bases; but a much longer text would include all of them, each one many times. Likewise, the text fragment in the middle panel contains only 18 of the 20 amino acids.

At the top panel of both the original Rosetta Stone and this drawing the alphabetical texts below are translated into a language where symbols have entire meanings, much as in ancient Chinese. In the drawing the meanings of the sequences of bases are now translated into the folded, functional shapes of an encoded protein.

The step from the bottom to the middle panel in this drawing is called the Genetic Code. Because there are 64 possible triplets of bases in a messenger RNA and only 20 amino acids the genetic code is redundant. Some amino acids are encoded by two, a few by four, and one by six different triplets.

Our own human genome has about 3 billion base-pairs. The protein-encoding parts make messages of various lengths, but at the high end a protein will not be much more than 10,000 amino-acids long, and a more typical size for a protein is in the range of 1000 amino-acids. So the genome has enough information to encode many different proteins.

# Figure 18

How many of those typical proteins could our genomes encode?

To get the answer, we divide the total number of base pairs in the genome ($3x10^9$) by the number of base pairs needed to encode a sequence of 1000 amino acids ($3x10^3$) to get $10^6$. So if the only function of the base pairs was to encode proteins, as many as one million different proteins of 1000 amino acids could be encoded. The obvious next step is to find out how many protein-coding sequences are actually in the human genome.

The unexpected answer is about ten or twenty thousand, no more than that. This discovery that so few different proteins can be assembled to make a person means that the information for encoding proteins takes up no more than one or two percent of the genome!

What then is going on with the remaining 98-99% of our genome? The earliest answer from genetics – which dealt with inherited differences we now know were differences in protein – was, nothing at all. The genteel scientists of fifty years ago called it non-coding DNA, the blunt ones called it junk DNA.

Today we know better. All but one or two percent of our genome is given over to gene regulation. Most – but not all – of the non-coding DNA in our genome is used for regulating whether or not a protein will be made from any one of those ten to twenty thousand coding sequences. The rest may not yet be well understood, but not many people today would call any of it junk.

Some stretches of the non-coding DNA are transcribed, not into messengers but to make non-coding regulatory RNAs that destroy specific messengers. Other stretches encode small RNAs that directly activate transcription of a messenger RNA; small RNAs can thus be either off- or on-switches.

In addition to the DNA encoding these regulatory RNAs, some of the proteins encoded by the genome also regulate transcription from a gene; sometimes it is their own transcription they regulate, sometimes the transcription of another gene, and sometimes the transcription of more than one gene. Finally some stretches of the genome serve in regulation simply by encoding a specific sequence to which regulatory proteins or RNAs may themselves bind.

The DNA of a person is organized in a sequence of texts much like the volumes of an encyclopedia. Scientists first saw the "volumes" of human DNA more than a century ago as separate human chromosomes. But because of gene regulation the DNA of a person is much more a set of programs than it is an encyclopedia, despite the coincidence of the 11th edition of the Encyclopedia Britannica coming in 23 volumes and a person's DNA being separated into 23 pairs of chromosomes.

In this drawing, the chromosomal location of a given stretch of DNA is no more than a bookmark for regulatory purposes. The DNA regulatory programs for different tissues are set aside as different volumes, not at all the same as the chromosomes in which they are found. The circuitry of regulation can reach across the entire genome to turn sets of genes on or off, so in regulatory terms the DNA encyclopedia is totally interactive.

# Figure 19

The DNA of a fish or a person is a catalog of programs for different tissues, with each tissue assembled by differential expression, and with expression of some genes unique to each tissue. With about $10^{14}$ cells in each of us, it must be the case that very few genes are transcribing precisely the same sequences at the same time in more than a small fraction of those cells. For example, expression of DNA sequences encoding the protein keratin are regulated to be active only in tissues that face the outside world such as skin, nails and hair.

But all the cells of a living person are the descendants of one fertilized egg cell and all carry the same exact DNA sequence, always copied by semi-conservative replication. What explains the cascades of differentiation that allow a fertilized egg – the first cell of what will grow into a plant or animal – to regulate its DNA transcription so that its two daughter cells, and all their progeny, are launched into different cascades of differentiation?

The initial regulatory program for making a multicellular organism is placed in the egg cell before fertilization, as that cell is itself matured by its own cascade of gene regulation.

In the assembly of a fully differentiated egg cell, regulatory RNAs and regulatory proteins are placed inside the cell in richly asymmetric patterns. On fertilization and with the first cell division of the fertilized egg, these regulatory molecules are distributed differently in that fertilized egg cell's descendent cells.

There they open a variety of cascades of differentiation that need not be the same in the daughter cells. As these play out, lineages of cells – all of them carrying copies of the same DNA of the fertilized egg – become increasingly different from each other.

The egg cell's guidance of the construction of a body from a single fertilized egg cell is a deep, subtle book of regulation. Here, protein synthesis is the introduction; the actual regulatory event is the immediate differences in gene regulation that occur in the daughter cells after fertilization of the egg. These show themselves as the emergence of what we see as an ever more complicated embryo from that fertilized egg, eventually becoming a fully functional individual organism.

Any form of life big enough to see is, we can now say, chemical, informationally rich, made of many cells, and fully differentiated into dozens or even hundreds of different tissues. All of that specialization into different tissues had occurred through cascades of differential gene expression. These differences in gene expression emerged with the first cell divisions after fertilization, according to the luck of the different regulatory molecules each new cell would capture from the fertilized egg.

Throughout life cascades of regulation also open to respond to many outside stimuli; we may experience these for instance as hunger or fullness; tiredness from lack of sleep or alertness upon awakening.

# Figure 20

How do regulatory circuits arise? We had initially equated mutation with a single base-pair change, because given enough time that simple event is enough in principle to explain the inheritance of any degree of novelty. Yet changing a single base-pair is only the simplest mutation.

Consider for instance the consequence of the machinery that is encoded by DNA for its own copying making another kind of mistake, by copying over a stretch of DNA so that one offspring DNA has more than one copy of that stretch. That error occurs often, as an unintended consequence of the fact that the two strands of DNA run in opposite directions. It is an error that can build on itself, so that two copies become four, four eight, and so on. When the stretch of DNA so mishandled contains an entire gene a large number of copies of that gene may accumulate.

In the large cells that appeared in the times recorded in volume 25, and then in the multicellular creatures assembled from large cells that followed soon after in the later times recorded in volumes 27 to 30, the genome within each cell had enlarged by gene duplication by about a thousand-fold, reaching billions of base-pairs per genome. When mutation would have its way, almost all of the copies in a gene family might be launched on different paths of mutational change over time while one copy would remain to provide the original function of the gene.

The baby is thus assembled from dots, because gene duplication and differential gene regulation assure that every part of its body was produced by a circuit of gene regulation unique to that part.

For example, there are three types of light-sensitive cells in the human retina that provide the nerve signals for color perception. The three types of cell differ in the protein portions of their respective light-sensitive molecules, called photopigments. Each shows a different peak sensitivity to the wavelengths of the visible spectrum of light.

The human capacity to distinguish yellowish red from yellowish green, regardless of the relative intensities of the two, comes from the different peak sensitivities of two of these molecules, erythrolabe and chlorolabe. If the gene for the erythrolabe protein or that for the chlorolabe protein does not function, then the capacity is lost: we have so called red/green color blindness.

There are two different types of red/green colorblindness depending on which gene is missing. So the question then becomes, why does everyone have light-sensitive cells with only one pigment protein active in each, even though overall, the genes for all three are present in every cell?

As our brains and eyes develop, gene regulatory circuits assure that a cell in the retina that will express one of these genes will not usually express the others. By that we can understand that normal human color discrimination is an example of a regulatory circuit that shuts off all but one member of the gene family in each cell, but a different gene is expressed in different types of receptor cells.

Now, why are there so many more red/green color-blind boys than girls?

# Figure 21

What a waste of genetic information we trade for sex at every generation! Egg, pollen and sperm must have one copy of any chromosome, and only one. That way the fertilized egg gets two copies for each chromosome, one from each parent. At each generation, having two parents means that the chromosome you got from your mother was one of two that she had gotten from her parents. Because you got that one, the other was lost.

And the same is true for the other parental chromosome of the pair: if you got, for instance, your father's mother's chromosome, you did not get, nor will you ever pass on, your father's father's version of that chromosome. There, in the instant of fertilization, half of the genetic information from each parent has been left behind.

What is the benefit of such a loss? You, and every individual that starts from egg and pollen or sperm, began life with a brand-new, never-before seen version of the DNA of its species. Not one, not two, but three shufflings of the chromosomal deck assure that happens at every generation.

First, before the sperm and egg are made, the chromosome pairs in the cells that will become sperm or egg line up and recombine, that is, they exchange DNA sequences. Second, every sperm, pollen and egg cell only gets one of the two parental versions of each chromosome; half the time that chromosome is itself a recombinant of sequences inherited by a parent from two grandparents. Third, each sperm or pollen and egg meets its partner entirely at random.

Recombination, random assortment, and random choice at fertilization together assure each member of a sexual species carries a truly novel version of its species' genome.

And now, why are boys more likely to be colorblind than girls? Boys are more at risk than girls because boys and girls differ in one of the twenty-three pairs of chromosomes that make up human DNA. In fact, one set is a pair only in girls. Girls have two X chromosomes, but boys only have one. The second X in a boy is replaced by a stubbier version, called a Y chromosome.

The genes for the erythrolabe and chlorolabe pigments needed for normal color vision lie next to each other on a chromosome called X. A girl will inherit one X from her mother and one X from her father. But a boy will inherit an X from his mother and another chromosome, called Y, from his father. Inheriting that mismatched pair of XY is why a boy's a boy.

In populations of European origin about 1 percent of X chromosomes lack the gene for erythrolabe and approximately another 1 percent lack the gene for chlorolabe. These failed genes occur throughout our species, though they are less frequent in populations of Asian and African origin.

Assuming the frequency is 1 percent, a boy has roughly a 2 percent chance of being red-green colorblind. For a girl to be colorblind she must have the same defective gene on both X chromosomes: $10^{-2} \times 10^{-2} = 10^{-4}$, or 0.01 percent, for erythrolabe, and likewise for chlorolabe.

So, red-green colorblindness is approximately 200 times less frequent in girls than in boys.

# Figure 22

Big cells built from billions of base-pairs of DNA must package it into segments – volumes – called chromosomes. Packaging is really too crude a word: chromosomes are tight coils of DNA wrapped around sets of proteins made from stretches of the DNA that encode them, with other regulatory proteins binding and unbinding the supercoiled state to allow or block transcription of a given gene.

Look again at those chromosomes – each is split up the middle. This is because each has been packaged after DNA replication, so each is actually carrying two full DNA copies of its sequence. When we see chromosomes in a dividing cell under the microscope they are in their most compacted state having been folded up for travel, that is, for distribution into each of two daughter cells as part of cell division.

Having two parents means there must be two sorts of cell division. The regular sort – called mitosis, simply grabs one of each copy of each chromosome and puts it into each of two new cells, each the genetic descendent of the original cell. Our bodies are built from mitosis coupled with gene regulation.

However meiosis, the sort of cell division that goes to make sperm, pollen and eggs, cannot put more than one copy of each chromosome into those cells because the fertilized egg may not have than two sets of chromosomes. So, as they line up for mitosis as at Stonehenge, each chromosome in a pair may look alike, but each in fact is from one of the organism's two parents.

But whether they have been doubled up and split down the middle for division by halves into two cells or are in their more dispersed state between cell divisions, each chromosome is also, as in the drawing, a single volume of the encyclopedic self-regulating text that is the genome of a given kind of multicellular life.

And like the monument at Stonehenge, a separate chromosome cannot participate in the full expression of its DNA contents except in the presence of all the others.

# Figure 23

Well before DNA was imagined by anyone at all, the monk Gregor Mendel cross-bred two inbred lines of peas whose pods and fruit were of distinctive colors. He closely observed the offspring peas in their pods. One line bred true with yellow peas, the other with green ones. Mendel could mate two pea plants to each other at will, by dusting the flower of one plant with the pollen of another. On crossing – F1 signifies the first filial generation of sons, a gender-based term we are stuck with – the offspring peas were all yellow.

Mendel called the yellow color the dominant version of what we would now call a single gene. The yellow color is the result of a single gene being able to make its protein successfully, while the green color results from the failure of a single gene to express itself, whether by regulation or by mutation.

A plant born from a pea that received one version of the relevant chromosome from a yellow-pea parent and one from the green-pea parent has yellow peas because it receives one copy of the functional gene, and one is enough to make the pea yellow. But this yellow pea makes a plant that has both kinds of gene for pea color, the functional one and the non-functional one.

So, when such "hybrid" yellow plants are bred to each other, each one of them has a 50% chance of donating a pollen or egg cell with a functional chromosome to the next generation, and 50% chance of donating one without a functional gene.

The result, as Mendel famously reported more than 150 years ago, is that on average one in four grandpeas of the initial cross between yellow-pea and green-pea parent plants, will receive two copies of the functional gene, two in four will get one copy of each version of the gene, and one in four will get two copies of the non-functional gene and be green.

**Figure 24**

Humans and peas both begin as fertilized eggs, so are a product of a hand dealt by fertilization at every generation; a random assortment of choices from the two parents, for every gene. Here's a mendelian example from our own families.

The red blood cells that bring oxygen to all the cells of our bodies have proteins on their surfaces that are encoded by two genes, one making a protein type A, and the other making a protein type B. Our red blood cells do not need either protein, and cells without either A or B are called type O. Like yellow for peas, blood-types A and B are both dominant; like green for peas, type O is recessive.

Since our parents may each have any two of these three possible versions of the gene for blood-type in each of their two paired chromosomes, they can pass many diferent combinations on to us. These combinations will be expressed as the presence on our red blood cells of one, or both, or neither of the proteins they encode. We call these different sets of proteins blood-types. There are four: A, B, AB and O, depending entirely on which versions we inherit from both parents for these two genes.

Consider the case of a woman with type A blood who has one chromosome with the gene for A and the other chromosome with the gene for O. She has two children fathered by a man with type B blood who has inherited one chromosome with the gene for B, and the other chromosome the gene for O as well. By the shuffle of egg and sperm formation and random assortment, along with the role of the dice at fertilization, their daughter has inherited the A from her mother and the B from her father. The son has inherited the O from both parents.

The mother exhibits blood-type A, the father blood-type B. And so, the hand this family has been dealt does not include the expression of either parental blood-type by either child. So much for inheritance by "blood," or "dilution."

# Chapter 3

**Figure 25**

DNAs found in nature are each very rare. That's because like any written message, any stretch of DNA represents a single possibility out of a great many. How rare is any single stretch of DNA? With four base-pairs possible at every position in the string, the number of possible DNA sequences of any size will be 4, multiplied by itself the same number of times as the length of the DNA string. So any single sequence of length N base-pairs, is one of $4^N$ possible sequences.

Note that the number of possible sequences rises much faster than the number of atoms used to make the DNA itself. A DNA stretch 3 base-pairs long is one of $4^3$ or 64 possible sequences. A stretch 6 base-pairs long is one of $4^6$ or 4096 possible sequences though it has only twice the number of atoms of the shorter one.

DNA information's rarity is a property of the length of a sequence, not of its subunits, just as the improbability of finding another person with your name is the consequence of the very large number of possible sequences of English letters that could be assembled in a string as long as a person's full name.

So how rare is the DNA of a gene, a chromosome, a bacterium, a big cell? Let's start small.

Imagine that a comic with a dull wit wears a poster-board that describes his performance: act a gag, act a gag, act. He tells you that that is also his name. He then tells you that you cannot have that name, because it belongs to him. He tells you not to worry, there's a sequence just for you, and a different one for everyone, just not this one.

And he then explains – he is not a good comic, but is a well-informed one – that his name is one of $4^{17}$ possible DNA stretches, each a different sequence of the four letters A, C, T and G. You do the calculation and find that $4^{17}$ is about $1.7 \times 10^{10}$.

That means there are more than 17 billion possible DNA stretches of that length, more than twice as many as there are people on the planet today.

# Figure 26

DNA sequences seventeen base-pairs long could be assigned to every person alive today and most likely to every person who ever lived as well. But naming people is not the way DNA works. It encodes information for transcription, regulation and translation. How long must a DNA sequence be to encode the survival of itself?

Viruses are the shortest sequences capable of copying themselves and also wrapping themselves in protein coats for survival. They can be very short because they are parasites of the cells in which they grow, using the cells' ribosomes and enzymes for their own replication. They are formidably aggressive, entering a cell and rapidly converting it into a factory for the production of themselves and then spilling out as the cell dies, ready to infect new cells for another round of murderous replication.

The information in a viral genome can be lethal to a cell that is so much more complex that a few billion base-pairs of information are necessary to keep it alive. So, as a bomb may kill a house and a barrage of rockets may destroy a town, the genomes of the smallest viruses are our most daunting competitors in the business of surviving.

DNAs for the smallest viruses, ones that can destroy a big and complicated cell the way these have, may have no more than a few thousand base-pairs in their DNAs. Their little genomes, smaller by millions-fold than our own genomes, are already capable of wreaking the havoc in Picasso's Guernica, bombing the little city of a cell out of existence.

How rare is a viral genome?

Any DNA sequence long enough to survive as a viral genome can be viewed as just a single possibility out of a vast number of sequences of that same length. For the genome of a small virus, there might be about 6000 base pairs, so that genome is one of $4^{6000}$ possibilities with that same length. This is about $10^{3600}$: a 1, followed by 3600 zeros. This number of possibilities is vastly larger than the estimated number of subatomic particles in the known universe (only about $10^{80}$).

How rare is a human genome?

The human genome, like most mammalian genomes, has about 3 billion base pairs rather than a mere 6000 for the virus: to write the number of possibilities in ordinary notation would require about 1,800,000,000 digits. At 10 digits per second, recording such a number would take over 5 years of nonstop printing.

Given the vast number of possible genomes this size, one might expect that the DNAs that characterize today's different tens of millions of different species would be very different from one another.

**Figure 27**

The DNA sequence of any of us is clearly unique in a very special way, emerging as it did from all those alternatives of the same length. Just one copy of it, though no longer than a meter, is one of so many possible sequences, that its uniqueness is hard to articulate. We cannot even begin to know the possibilities opened by other sequences that long nor even to list them; they are effectively infinite in number.

That is the true natural underpinning of what every person has always known from direct experience: every individual is equally rare and equally precious and should be treasured while they are with us. All of us are unimaginably rare, absolutely unique at birth.

The particular sequences that make up each person's version of the human genome will not come about again. With $10^{14}$ cells each enfolding DNA that is about a meter long, the unique DNA in any person would be $10^{11}$ kilometers long if laid end to end. That would extend from Earth to the outer planets.

Compared to the paltry $10^{25}$ molecules of water in the mug of ocean water, a few of which would be fished out in the second dip into the oceans, no amount of random dilution and mixing would ever fish out a sequence even slightly similar to any of our DNAs from the sea of all possible DNA sequences capable of encoding a human being.

In this sense, each member of a pair of twins is no less rare than any person born alone.

How then can it be that all living things share DNA sequences?

# Figure 28

Given the incomprehensible rarity of every sequence big enough to form a genome, and given the existence of hundreds of millions of species today, each with its own species-genome and a unique version of the species genome in each of its members, we might presume that the genomes that characterize each of today's species would be completely different from one another.

About twenty years ago this presumption became testable by direct sequencing of the DNA of many species. Three discoveries stood out from the very first experiments:

First, all species' DNAs contain regions of similarity or identity with all other species' DNAs. That is a bit surprising, but could easily be explained by DNA traveling from one species to another, carried along in the genome of an infectious virus or bacterium.

But second, species that are as incommensurately different as frog and peach, beetle and elephant, roach and rose, or even chimp and professor, have overall sequence similarities in their genomes that range between 98% for the professor and the chimp, down to a small but real overlap of sequences even for the roach and the rose or the beetle and the elephant.

Third and most remarkably, the few percent of the DNA of each species given over to protein coding are much more similar from species to species than the more typical sequences involved in regulation. For instance, taking our own version of a given protein as the model it turns out that the amino-acid sequence of a protein is the same to within a tenth of a percent in a chimp's DNA; the same within 1 percent in our DNA and in the DNA of a dog; and 60% similar in our DNA and the DNA of a fly.

So, it seems we are presented with a real puzzle: why are DNA sequences in all these species and by extension in all species related to one rather than being distributed evenly though the vast informational richness of all possible long DNA sequences?

The solution is simply to beg the question and say: the DNAs of all species are related to one another. And then, because of the fact of semi-conservative replication of DNA, the penny can drop.

If all current DNAs are related to one another, it becomes possible to imagine that all current species have a common ancestor.

**Figure 29**

If DNA can encode its own replication why has life on Earth become this complicated? Why are there so many kinds of life? Why not just one, perfect, self-copying machine? It would be alive after all; why do so many enormously complicated genomes all survive in so many species today, instead?

Let's go back to the Bayeux Tapestry of land vertebrates in figure 7. There are many species there, but they are not in a parade. The Bayeux Tapestry itself is the record of a struggle for survival, one barely won by the British at Hastings. So too in nature, as Darwin saw, there are struggles for survival of species, with unpredictable outcomes.

As DNA copies itself by semiconservative replication, a change in sequence may be preserved and then copied into the future, until it is changed again by another mutation. Darwin called the small differences in the genomes of individuals within a species "inherited variations" and he noted that they are the sole source of novelty contributing to the survival of the population over time.

Let's consider how this might work in terms of semi-conservative DNA replication. The copying of a DNA sequence requires a lot of energy and many machines made of protein and RNA. Genes for these machines are, of course, among the sequences encoded in any DNA capable of self-replication; that's how that capability is gained.

Now consider the next question: errors and their repair are making a host of new sequences over time, as the encoded machinery for copying DNA bumbles along. What if one or more of those mutational changes improves the quality of the copying?

Maybe it makes the copying go faster; maybe it makes it more accurate; maybe it just makes it work better in some other, undecipherable way. The long-term consequence of any novelty that enhances its own copying is to give the novel sequence a leg up into the future. Over time, all other things held constant, that new sequence should replace its ancestral one as well as all others that cannot compete for the copying of themselves.

This is the answer to the diversity of life in a DNA-based living world: a positive feedback loop rewards any sequence change capable of enhancing its own replication, and gives it hegemony over all ancestral sequences and other variants arising at the same time. It becomes the new normal sequence.

Of course, "normal" depends on where you live. So, sequences whose links to successful DNA survival were only distantly linked to its replication might also contribute to the survival of the life-form they encoded.

Any change that would allow a version of life to survive, would survive within that version of life. Ancestral DNA is a track, with a switch-point in the railway for the survival of two different life forms. The set of DNA changes a train would have to accumulate to run down one track would preclude going down the other.

# Figure 30

How does the notion of this positive feedback loop apply to us and the other species of things big enough to see, the species that first arose from big cells and gained the additional sequence shuffling of sexual reproduction soon afterward? The ancient loop would be expected to reward DNA sequences involved in survival of a species genome by giving individuals born with them a preference at survival under some particular set of conditions. But consider the possibility that would arise whenever a change in those conditions meant that a small population within a successful species became physically or behaviorally separated from the rest.

The loop would continue to operate in the larger population, and also in the separated one. With time the changes that contributed to survival under these different conditions might be expected to diverge in the two populations. Consider next what would happen if the loop rewarded one set of changes in DNA with survival in one subpopulation, and another set of DNA changes with survival in the other.

Eventually there might come a time when even if descendants of the two sub populations tried to mate, their offspring would be unable to survive due to the differences in DNA sequence accumulating over time in the two separated populations. Each might still be the source of its own offspring, each would still be able to mate and bring forth a new generation in turn. That is to say, that a species might eventually be the source of a new species.

The new species would have a genome very reminiscent of the one it had branched off from. In fact any single cell of any species has in its nucleus a genome that encodes not only the information for the construction and viability of an individual of that species, but also a record of its ancestry, in which those sequences that continue to work well enough under its own particular circumstances are preserved. In that, the nucleus is like the site of the ancient Temple in the walled city of Jerusalem.

We see our species' history retained in the construction of our own bodies: early human embryos and early fish embryos look remarkably alike, because the parts of each genome given over to the regulation of gene expression in early embryogenesis have been preserved for a billion years or more, since we and fishes had one last common ancestral vertebrate in the seas.

All random mutations that would have occurred and changed the functions of those regulatory sequences in the ancestral species and in all the intermediate species that lived and died over that billion years, would have disappeared because no changed function would have been able to compete with the one we share with the fishes today.

# Figure 31

Charles Darwin imagined this consequence of a positive feedback loop that selected for different variations under different conditions more than 150 years ago, a hundred years before DNA's capacity to copy itself was understood.

His initial report of this insight, published as a brief book in 1853, gives the entire story away in its title: *The Origin of Species*. Not *The Origin of Life*, about which he had no observations from nature, but the origin of species. By that he means to say, species have an origin; they are not eternal. In one short title he claimed for the living world a radical changeability.

The origin of a species had to have been an earlier species, now dead and perhaps fossilized in the ground. His idea is presented here in a way that honors his prescience while recognizing the positive feedback loop in DNA replication that is its mechanism.

The feedback loop of DNA change that enhances DNA survival is represented here by a slot machine. The handle of the slot machine is a chromosome and the spinning wheels are ancestral species. They have rolled and come up with three ancestral mammals, from a species that might have died out a hundred million years ago.

The elephant, boar, anteater, dog, seal and bat are a sampling of the winners, today's species of mammals.

**Figure 32**

We honor Darwin's profound insight by showing here a facsimile of Darwin's own notes from the moment of his understanding. From that moment until now, the notion of time in human terms has been radically altered by the fact of "deep time." "Deep time" is the billions of years that preceded the Earth's formation, and the billions more that preceded the emergence by natural selection of the forms of life – the mammals – that include ourselves.

Here, his note to mark the moment is not mounted as a page in a book, but as the face of a clock. That clock was ticking for more than 13 billion years, but its face was hidden until the moment of this drawing.

He writes "I think" and then draws a tree. The base of it, numbered "1," is a hypothetical ancestor of all the species that make up the tree.

The length of a limb is the length of time since a branching.

Each branching is the emergence of a new species from an older one.

All the species alive today have a crossbar; the other ancestral ones at every branching are dead and with luck remembered both as ancestors and as fossils.

To look at the species alive today, B, C and D would appear recognizably similar, but A would be quite different; think of a Boy, a Chimp, a Dog and an Albatross.

We see that B, C and D all have a recent common ancestor at the base of their branches. A on the other hand is not in that cluster, but it does share a common ancestor with the other three living species.

The generality is stunning: all forms of life are mortal. No matter how different, they share their current viability and their common ancestry but only the latter is permanent.

**Figure 33**

Darwin's tree has stretched and filled out by 150 years of study. Darwin had no clue that for almost all of the time of life on Earth, it had taken the form of bacteria, small cells, too small to see. His "1" turns out to be a long, long trunk of a tree of life, with the branches representing life forms big enough to see crowning the bacterial trunk only in the past billion years.

Today we know it is rooted in the archeobacteria, whose ancestors are about four billion years old.

Most of its leaves – the species alive today – are still too small to see. In that sense, what worked first still works best.

Off one branch are all the animals big enough to see. A squirrel runs down the branch of mammals. The branch with no living species – leaves – was the dinosaurs; branching off from its base is the twig of today's birds.

When someone asks, "when does life begin" the answer is, "It never begins, it only ends; life having begun once has persisted until now." Lives however do end, and that is the price exacted by that kernel of regulation, the positive feedback loop that rewards the successful genome with survival.

It is after all, a mindless circuit that rewards not goodness nor kindness, but only fecundity and survival itself.

Semiconservative DNA replication has always been coupled to the positive feedback loop that rewards a mutational difference with its own survival in a genome whenever that difference assists in the survival and replication of the DNA encoding it. Darwin's vision of a single tree of life is this positive feedback loop applied to all species.

Each leaf of a species has emerged from an earlier species as mutational differences in its species DNA led to enhanced survival of members of the species under some particular set of circumstances. As Darwin saw, those circumstances include the interaction of members of every species with all others in a given time and place; today we call the study of particular times and places and the species interactions occurring there the science of ecology.

And where does that leave us?

# Figure 34

Differences in sequence accumulate in a genome over time. By comparing genomes of different species alive today, we can measure how different they are. If the positive feedback loop of natural selection working to preserve some mutations in DNA sequence through semi-conservative replication is a sufficient explanation for the Darwinian model of the origin of species, we can make a dramatic prediction. We should find that the more different two species' DNAs are today, the longer ago it was that they had the same common ancestral species.

For a stretch of DNA encoding a protein, not all novelties of mutational change in a single base-pair need necessarily have any effect at all on the final functional protein. The ones that have no effect because the genetic code is redundant are called neutral mutations. They will accumulate in any DNA over time without effect, and so provide a clock by which to measure how long ago the DNA molecules from two different related organisms might have diverged from a single species genome.

All ancestral species are dead. We can only compare the degree of similarity of the fossils of ancestral species with the current bodily structures of today's species. The comparison remarkably and wonderfully confirms the prediction. It is indeed the case that the more different two species' genomes are, the older the fossils of their last common ancestor species are. This allows us to draw the tree of common ancestry with a three-dimensional vision informed both by fossil and DNA evidence.

As a species, we're one of tens of millions of species alive today, an ordinary living twig on the great bushy top of the long spindly tree of life. Nested first within the doll of our species, Homo sapiens – the thinking species – is another primate species' genome, to show that our two are most closely similar because we share a most recent common ancestor.

Nested inside that primate genome is the genome of a bird, a more distant cousin. Inside of all of them is the genome of a reptile and then a mammal, to represent the period of hundreds of millions of years when ancestral species of both lived together, with the reptilian species so much larger that we think of that period as the age of dinosaurs.

And then as the dolls get smaller and the tree fades into the past we find three nested genomes of an ancestral insect, fish, and arthropod. These last two are nested around a paramecium to represent the large single-celled forms of life from which all the others then emerged in not much more than a billion years.

# Chapter 4

**Figure 35**

Let's go back to that outermost, biggest Russian doll which represents our own human genomes. In this drawing a pointillist baby sits surrounded by the chromosomal information from which it grew by gene regulation, happy with its toys and perhaps thinking its first unencoded thoughts.

Measured against the 2 billion or more years of life the entire set of dolls represents, our genomes are remarkably new, and our numbers are remarkably large. The last ancestor common to all of today's primates – including us – died off about 35 million years ago. Since 20 million years is only 1 percent of 2 billion years that means the first primates appeared after more than 99% of the time that big-celled life has been present on Earth.

Our closest primate relative is the chimp. The difference between our species genome and the chimp genome is only a few percent, and almost all of that is in regulatory regions of our respective DNAs. Humans and chimps are built more or less from the same protein bricks and stones; it is the architectural plans for regulatory DNA that have been changed by natural selection since our last common ancestor species died off about 7 million years ago.

Seven million years is a very short time for those regulatory sequence changes to have been selected. The result of this burst of concerted selection has been to give us DNA sequences in regions that have remained unchanged since the last common ancestor of birds and mammals. Those sequences that are changed in us and otherwise the same in all other mammals and birds give us particularly human inherited qualities.

Such anatomically inherited qualities are easy to tick off: a bigger brain; a brain that matures slowly, leaving the human infant helpless and in need of close caring for years rather than weeks; a set of hands with thumbs that allow complicated manipulations of objects; a changed anatomy of throat and mouth that allows for a vast complexity of sounds we call speech; and most significantly, a new positive feedback loop that links them together.

Our enormous success at forming multiple overlapping social groups for the teaching and learning from each other throughout life has enabled us to use these human-specific mutational differences to construct mental worlds of novel complexity.

Our most recent ancestral species all lived in Africa and so did our first human ancestors, for most of those millions of years. Tempting though it is to imagine that this history is also one of progress toward some sort of equilibrium, it appears that the first fully modern humans were the survivors of a history of natural selection in which each pre-human species seems to have survived the death of all its predecessors.

Our species accomplished that most recently after leaving Africa to cover the planet, with the death of the Neanderthal hominid species in Europe some tens of thousands of years ago.

Novel mental complexity has not always meant kindness and generosity.

# Figure 36

Our burst of growth as a species began about sixty thousand years ago when small populations of humans left Africa to migrate north to Europe, central Asia, east Asia and then Polynesia. Eventually, approximately fifteen thousand years ago, humans migrated over the Bering straits to the Americas, making final landfall in the tip of South America in the past ten thousand years.

And now, here we are. Seven billion of us cover the entire globe and are changing it forever. We speak thousands of languages, invent music, art, science, law, philosophy, economics, sports and games, and religions. Our brains record memories that can be shared and so last a lifetime and more; we imagine thousands of reasons for every event we experience and every feeling we have.

Darwin called the human mind "an excrescence of the brain" and counted our unique mental capacities among the rewards of natural selection for us as a species. So on a foundation of neural circuitry we have built temples in our mind, often with a personification, like Athena, of a wisdom we hope we may attain. What a great success natural selection has found in us!

Or, perhaps not. Our mental worlds are no longer subject to natural selection. In fact, they never were; that's the reason for our spectacularly dispro-portionate success at proliferating. We have broken out of natural selection's slow sieve of mutation; we can simply have an idea, and choose to act on it. No need to wait for natural selection's positive feedback loop to select for a DNA variation that permits that new idea. Any brain can have any idea, any time.

So the joke of our imagination is on nature, but as a consequence it is on us as well. Our minds can encompass nature, but they can also go beyond nature, and imagine things that need not be possible in nature. When we do that, we may escape nature for a while, but in the end, these excrescences of the brain will be brought back into alignment with the facts of nature by the fact of species mortality. If there is one place for imagination to generate wisdom, that would be the place.

# Figure 37

One of the first basic biology experiments to take advantage of a novel DNA sequence's capacity to express itself in a living thing was the insertion of a sequence encoding a green fluorescent protein into the genome of a fertilized frog egg. The GFP gene was inserted next to the regulatory region of a protein made only in a single tissue of the frog. The frog was born as happy as any, and seemed not to care that when it was illuminated with blue light that tissue fluoresced a bright green. From such experimentations we have begun to map the regulatory circuitry of our own embryonic development.

That early research was done a while ago, before computers had flat screens and before those screens were also in everyone's pocket. A frog still cannot edit its own DNA, but now a person can. There are lots of reasons for the difference. But the one of most interest to us is our ability to manipulate texts and meanings in our minds. Our minds are much faster than our DNA.

Let's take this sentence: "A sequence of base pairs encodes the data of a gene storing information on the text of life," and mutate it, one letter at a time, to see if we can go from base to data to gene to text to life without ever losing the meaningfulness of the intermediate words. That would be a fair representation of natural selection's capacity to go from sequence to sequence, rewarding the new meaning by its survival, without ever going through a lethal mutation to meaninglessness.

When I taught this notion in a first-year class at Columbia University, I gave the following string of mutational changes, one letter at a time as my best effort, my fastest evolution from Base to Life by mental, not natural, selection: BASE bale dale date DATA date Dane cane cant cent gent GENE gent tent TEXT tent cent cant cane lane line LIFE. It took 21 mutational, meaningful steps, including a few back-mutations.

I told my class to send me an email with any faster path if anyone could come up with one. An hour later, back in my office, a student had sent me this: BASE bale dale date DATA date Dane dine dint dent gent GENE gent tent TEXT test lest list lift LIFE.

This new path took 19 mutations, a ten percent shortening, and it took one hour to be thought through by a student who was not yet 20 years old. Within a few weeks a second, even shorter path arrived in the mail, sent by a student in a fifth-grade science class who had attended a similar lecture at his school. Compare the emergence of a new meaningful pathway of informational mutation in a matter of hours or days to the time it takes for any single DNA change in our genomes to show itself in the next generation.

There are 24 x 365 = 8760 hours in a year. The human generation time is about twenty years. So, human mental selection is tens of thousands of times faster than DNA and natural selection.

**Figure 38**

The Mayan civilization began about ten thousand years ago with the arrival of the first humans in Central America. It was taken down by invaders from Europe about five hundred years ago. No doubt the invaders regarded themselves as more advanced than these Mayans who did not speak a civilized European language, nor worship a European notion of divinity.

But the Mayans were a religious people, and the drawing of a Mayan stele compels us to remember them and to imagine what they might have made of our current capacity to manipulate the sequences within the DNA of many species, including our own.

Ringed by the DNA double helix, the monument shows, on the right, the corn that humans had selected by their own weeding and breeding from a native grass. Below it, the emergence of a local medicine, informed by the human capacity to teach and learn about the risks and benefits of one or another plant or animal. And then on the left, a series of panels were carved to show the consequences of the human ability to manipulate the sequence of a DNA.

First, we see a panel showing the new human capacity to bring the fertilization of sperm and egg out of the body and into a dish. Just below it there is a representation of our forty-year-old ability to move pieces of DNA encoding genes of interest from one genome to another.

Below we see what appear to be a rodent and a cow, to represent a mouse and a cow that have received through DNA recombination in the laboratory the gene of a person or a fly or a bacterium. And finally, at the bottom, a representation of our ability – available in principle but unusable because we know it to be wrong – to change the DNA of a fertilized egg in order to generate a baby with a novel mental capacity in its brain.

**Figure 39**

The technology of transmission of a string of sounds has changed very rapidly in the past century.

The record player encoded a symphony or speech or song as a spiral track on a flat plastic disc. Like a stretch of DNA, that spiral could be decoded, but as sound through translation by vibrating needle into a set of electrical impulses which drove a vibrating cone in a speaker.

The recording of life has played out through the amplifier of natural selection for more than four billion years. We now have a lot of reasons to be concerned about its future.

For the past 11,000 years we have lived on a planet sufficiently stable that geologists call the period by a single name, the Holocene epoch. Now they debate whether our species' impact on our planet has been sufficiently degrading and irreversible to warrant the establishment of a new geological epoch, the Anthropocene.

Markers of human-initiated change run through the Earth's water, air, land and life. In the past century the oceans have become more acidic as they take up the extra carbon dioxide we have put into the air by our appetite for the burning of fossil fuels. Global average temperature has risen in step with that additional $CO_2$. All seven continents now show signs of erosion and intensive usage by our species, as woodlands, grasslands, steppes, shrublands, deserts and tundras become subject to our wish to manage, maintain and change them for our purposes.

At the beginning of the Holocene humans numbered in the millions. We along with our domesticated animals made up about 0.1% of the total biomass of mammals. Today our numbers are about $10^3$-fold higher at 7 billion, and approximately 90% of the mammalian biomass is made up of us and our domesticated species.

These numbers mark both a geological epoch and also a change in tune. Is the Anthropocene going to last 11,000 years as well? In geological terms it is hard to see how our planet can continue for much longer to carry the burden of our species' success at bypassing natural selection, whether expressed through our mental activity or our capacity for joint action at the largest scales, or both.

The adjustment, if it comes through natural selection, will undoubtedly be a problem for our species. After all, because Darwin's vision of natural selection still applies to us all even with our mental worlds, we will either survive as a species or not. Either way, chances are that DNA-based life will go on.

Our difference is, of course, that our mental capacities and our capacities for joint action do give us a unique extra capacity to control our future, a capacity we do not share with any other known creature on Earth. We are not merely a song on this record; we can make our own recordings.

Let's hope we use that power wisely.

**Figure 40**

The philosophers speak of four kinds of love, each having its place in the life of a person. Eros, for desire; Agape, for unconditional love; Filia, for family and friendship; and Caritas, for love and kindness to the stranger.

Let's close this book the way we opened it, with a thought about questions, and with the certainty that as no species will live forever, no question will have a final answer. Neither a DNA sequence in nature, nor any sequence we may construct and test in our laboratories or our farms will ever be fully knowable in advance of natural selection's capacity to favor it or kill it.

Does this mean we must give in to cynicism, or to despair? If there is one lesson we can take from our DNA sequences and the tapestry of our origins by natural selection, it is this: cynicism and despair are choices, but not ones encoded by our DNA. But these four kinds of love are encoded, and they can be expressed by any of us through our lifetimes.

None of us could have begun without Eros. None of us could have survived the burden of our inherited late-maturing neural circuitry without Agape from someone who cared for us at a time when we were of no use nor value except for our lovability. None of us could begin to understand the world and our chance of happiness in it without Filia. None of us can be fully human without Caritas, both from us and to us.

From that baseline gift of nature, it seems to us a small step to read the book of our origins in nature as allowing us – if not encouraging us – to choose to treat others only in the way we'd wish ourselves to be treated in turn.

# Acknowledgements

We could not have drawn and written this book without the help of a number of people.

We thank Columbia Professors Darcy Kelley, David Helfand and Don Hood and course administrator Elina Yuffa for inviting us to assemble and present the very first version of this book as a set of three lectures to the first-year students of Columbia College in the Core course "Frontiers of Science."

We thank Catherine Macaulay, science teacher at Hunter College Elementary School, for asking us to present a shortened but no less rigorous version of those lectures to her class in what was an astonishingly intense seminar with two dozen ten-year-olds.

We thank our daughter Marya for reading the manuscript in its earliest version, her entire family for encouraging us both to see this through, and, in particular, our grandson for his editorial contributions.

We thank our student colleague Emma Chaves for the insight described in the legend to Figure 37 and for many incidences of kindness since.

We thank Summer and Connery Hart, Cynthia Peabody, Barak Wouk, Andrew Sinanoglou, Nathan Ashe, Miranda Hawkins, Susan and Ken Schept, Dawn Digrius, John Horgan, John McCaskey, John Loike, Pilar Jennings, David Kagan, Trevor Marshall, Gessy Alvarez, Alice and Rob Newton, Meredith and Michael Bergmann, Allison Levin, Katie Gerbner, and Sean Blanchet for encouragement and for reviewing earlier versions of the drawings and helping us to make ourselves clearer.

We thank CAL Dean and Stevens Professor of Philosophy Lisa Dolling and Columbia Professor of Psychology David Krantz who together also gave us good advice and in addition envisioned this book and its purposes even before we did.

We thank University Seminars Archivist Summer Hart for preparing both figures and text for publication and Stevens Professor Ed Foster for advice in publishing this edition, with support to both from Professor Krantz's remarkable gift to CAL.

We reserve for ourselves responsibility for all that is in this book, and hope the reader will join the circle of those who have helped us by letting us know of errors and misunderstandings.

*Amy and Robert Pollack*